```
612.6     Ask about who I am
A834
```

LEAVENWORTH LIBRARY

Who I Am

This edition first published in 1987 by Raintree Publishers Inc.

Text copyright © 1987 by Raintree Publishers Inc., translated by Alison Taurel.
© 1983 Hachette

All rights reserved. No part of this book may be reproduced or utilized in any form or by any means, electronic or mechanical including photocopying, recording, or by any information storage and retrieval system without permission in writing from the publisher. Inquiries should be addressed to Raintree Publishers Inc., 310 West Wisconsin Avenue, Milwaukee, Wisconsin 53203.

Library of Congress Number: 86-33870

1 2 3 4 5 6 7 8 9   94 93 92 91 90 89 88 87

Library of Congress Cataloging in Publication Data

Baradeau, Christiane.
    Ask about who I am.

    Translation of: Dis moi qui je suis.
    Summary: Answers questions about the origin of life, identity, and the purpose of life and living.
    1. Human reproduction—Juvenile literature.
    2. Life (Biology)—Juvenile literature.   3. Identity (Psychology)—Juvenile literature.   [1. Reproduction. 2. Life (Biology)   3. Identity.   4. Questions and answers]   I. Title.
QP251.5.B3713   1987   612.6   86-33870
ISBN 0-8172-2883-7 (lib. bdg.)
ISBN 0-8172-2895-0 (softcover)

Cover illustration: David Schweitzer

Ask About
Who I Am

RAINTREE PUBLISHERS
Milwaukee

Contents

I, myself

Why do I like looking at my baby pictures? 8
Is it better to be a boy or a girl? 8
Where was I before I was born? 10
Why was I born? 10
How come I was the one to be born? 10
Why do children like to sleep with teddy bears or dolls? 12
What are dreams? 12
What is a nightmare? 12
Why do people scare themselves by telling stories about witches and ghosts? 14
What about stories with giants, ogres, or huge wolves? 14
Fairy tales are not meant to be frightening. What is their purpose? 14
When you want something very much, can you make it happen? 16
Can other people read your thoughts? 16
Why do I cry when I am sad? 16
Why do people blush? 18
Why do I have to go to school? 18
Why do some children suck their thumbs, and why don't grown-ups like it? 18
Why do I feel like breaking things when I am angry? 20
What does it mean to feel depressed? 20
Why do people make fun of people who are different? 20
Why do I want to do bad things sometimes? 22
Why do children sometimes want to be mean to their new baby brother or sister? 22
What does "jealous" mean? 22
What is love? 24
What is hate? 24
Why are some people beautiful and some people ugly? 24
When I am finished growing, will I start over and become small again? 26
Why do we live? 26
What is happiness? 26

I, my family

Why can't I sleep in the same room as my parents? 28
How does someone find a husband or a wife? 28
Is it bad to like one parent more than the other? 30
Do people ever get married when they are very young or when they are very old? ... 30
What is the kind of love that I have for my brother or sister? 30
Do parents always love their children? 32
Do children love their parents forever? 32
Do parents love each other forever? 32
Why do parents get angry with their children? 34
Do parents ever hit their children? 34
Can a child talk back to a parent? 34
Why do children have to obey their parents? 36
Can young children spend the day having adventures in new places
without any grown-ups? 36
Should children run away from home? 36
Why do grandparents like to talk about the good old days? 38
Are grandparents going to die? 38
Will I be very sad when someone I love dies? 38
Why do people die? 40
Why is there a funeral when people die? 40
When people are buried, what happens to them? 40

I, others

Why do people live in cities? 42
Why do I have to share? 42
Why do I have to be nice to people when I don't want to be? 44
Why do I have to be polite? 44

What does it mean to behave? 44
Why is it so much fun to pretend? 46
Why is playing "dress up" so much fun? 46
Why don't grown-ups play very much? 46
Do others know when I am telling a lie? 48
Do grown-ups always tell the truth? 48
Do parents have secrets? 48
Why can't I watch television all the time? 50
Why do I have to go to bed early? 50
Why do grown-ups say bad words but won't let children say them? 50
Why do children need to learn how to use knives, forks, and spoons? 52
Why can't I only eat food that I like? 52
Why can't I be mean to other children? 52
How come grown-ups smoke cigarettes even though they know that
it is bad for them? 54
Why do people drink alcohol? 54
Why do some people waste food when other people are starving? 54
How do I choose a job? 56
Do I have to work when I grow up? 56
Can children earn money? 56
Can children go to jail? 58
Why is there crime? 58
Why are some people unhappy? 58
Will I learn everything I am to know in school? 60
Do I have to like school? 60
Why do children like to ask so many questions? 60

Glossary 62
Index 63

I, myself

Why do I like looking at my baby pictures?

You have changed since you were the little baby in those photographs. You have grown and learned how to walk and talk. You are getting to know yourself. You are finding out about your thoughts and feelings. Your parents can tell you about things that you used to do. You look at the photographs and say, "Tell me who I am."

Is it better to be a boy or a girl?

Girls' lives and boys' lives are somewhat different, but neither one is better. Each is worthwhile especially if you put your whole heart into living your life.

Where was I before I was born?

Before your parents had you, you did not exist as you are now. Your eyes, your hair—your entire body—did not have form. Your parents joined together to give you your life.

Why was I born?

You were born because a man and a woman loved each other. It takes two people to make a child. These people are your parents.

How come I was the one to be born?

One of your father's seeds among many others joined a small egg in your mother's body to form you. No one can choose the personality or looks of a child or choose if the child will be a boy or a girl. At your birth, there was both the surprise and the joy for your loved ones of getting to know a brand new human being. You are unique and different in all the world.

Why do children like to sleep with teddy bears or dolls?

It's late, and the sun has disappeared. It's time to go to bed. You get your teddy bear, a doll, or a favorite blanket to hold tightly while falling asleep. These familiar things help children go from the daytime world into dreamland. The teddy or other snuggly object keeps you company. It reassures you, and you can fall peacefully asleep.

What are dreams?

When you relax and go to sleep, you sometimes enter the world of dreams. Your brain invents this world and it tells you stories. It can take you through time and space and give you the most extraordinary adventures all in your mind. Each person has their own individual dreams which reflect innermost thoughts.

What is a nightmare?

Perhaps you have awakened in the middle of the night crying. One of your parents may have come in to comfort you and to ask you what happened. You probably had a nightmare or a bad dream. When you woke up, you were frightened and felt terrible; but you probably were also glad to be safe in your bed.

Why do people scare themselves by telling stories about witches and ghosts?

Stories about witches and ghosts are frightening but also very entertaining because the stories are exciting! They can make you tremble and squeal. At the conclusion of the story, you may burst out laughing because it is such a relief to have the story finished!

What about stories with giants, ogres, or huge wolves?

In the eyes of a child, a grown-up might seem like a giant. A mean grown-up might remind you of an ogre. A noise in the night might become a huge wolf in your imagination. These kinds of stories can be scary, but they can serve to relieve you of your fears once the storytelling is through.

Fairy tales are not meant to be frightening. What is their purpose?

These stories were made up a very long time ago. Fairy tales are filled with kings and queens, wizards, magical kingdoms, and talking animals. Fairy tales are fun, and they teach important things about life. A well-known fairy tale is "The Ugly Duckling" by Hans Christian Andersen. It is the story of a duckling that none of the other animals liked because it was so ugly. But the duckling eventually turns into a magnificently beautiful swan.

When you want something very much, can you make it happen?

If you tried very hard to fly with your arms or to turn a person into a frog, you could not do it. Some wishes are possible, however. If you want to become an explorer, a magician, or a doctor when you grow up, you can achieve it if you work very hard. Some grown-ups have attained the dreams that they had as children.

Can other people read your thoughts?

When you think about something, no one else knows what you are really thinking about. Someone could guess what you are thinking, however, by the expression on your face. People can probably tell from looking at you whether you are happy or furious. But what is really going on inside your head is your secret. The only way that people will know your thoughts is if you tell them what they are.

Why do I cry when I am sad?

Believe it or not, crying is actually good for you! When you are in pain or feel sad, your body is affected. It is hard to swallow, your chin trembles, and your tears flow. Crying helps you express your unhappiness or pain and hopefully eases the problems that you are having. It is interesting to discover that people not only cry from sadness, but from anger, rage, and joy.

Why do people blush?

Blushing is the reaction that some people have when they become irritated or embarrassed. Shy people blush often. The feelings that they have on the inside show themselves on the outside, and their faces become pink or red.

Why do I have to go to school?

Some children enjoy school but others don't. It is important for all children to attend their classes, however. An education is necessary if you are to get along in the world. Everyone needs to know how to read, write, do mathematics, and know about our earth in order to live a productive life. A good education can also mean that you will be able to get a job that you enjoy when you grow up.

Why do some children suck their thumbs, and why don't grown-ups like it?

Adults say to a child, "Don't suck your thumb!" They say this even though they may smoke cigarettes, which is a much more harmful habit. Sucking your thumb can bring pleasure, comfort, and reassurance. Both thumb sucking and cigarette smoking are bad habits that people should try to stop.

Why do I feel like breaking things when I am angry?

When you are very angry, you are overcome with emotion. You think you might be able to get rid of some of your anger by breaking things. You may get more frustrated, however, when you find that you have broken something special or expensive.

What does it mean to feel depressed?

Everyone feels depressed from time to time. You feel tired, sad, and perhaps lonely. Depression can be caused by many things. Maybe there has been a death in your family, or maybe your best friend has just moved away. Depression can come, too, if you do not get enough sleep, sunlight, and exercise, or if you do not eat healthy food.

Why do people make fun of people who are different?

Some people are frightened by people who are different in any way. Some people make fun of others who behave strangely, who are handicapped, or who look unusual. It is rude to make fun of people who are different. If you'd get to know the person, you'd probably find that he or she is very nice.

Why do I want to do bad things sometimes?

Most people have an aggressive part to their personalities. It makes them want to do nasty things from time to time. But causing trouble can bring you trouble, too. It is best to get your aggression under control. Sports or playing hard helps release a little of your "steam."

Why do children sometimes want to be mean to their new baby brother or sister?

Jealousy might make you want to be mean to your baby brother or sister. Before the new baby was born, perhaps you were the one who got all the attention. After the baby arrived, you had to share your parents' time and attention. Maybe you feel like you will be forgotten forever, and this makes you unhappy and mean.

What does "jealous" mean?

Being jealous means that you are upset that you are not the person getting the attention or that you don't have something that someone else has such as a new toy, a model car, a computer, or blond, curly hair.

What is love?

There is a difference between loving cake and loving a person. To love a person is to listen to the feelings in your heart and to reach out. Loving makes people want to live and to share their happiness.

What is hate?

Hate is the opposite of love. It is a powerful feeling. One kind of hate is very destructive. It makes you want to harm someone or do damage to something. Another kind of hate is the hatred of bad things in the world such as war, poverty, or prejudice. One more form of hate is the personal dislike for something such as spinach or going to the dentist.

Why are some people beautiful and some people ugly?

This happens by chance, but the only kind of beauty that counts is the beauty found on the inside of people. Everyone is beautiful when they are filled with love. It makes your eyes twinkle and shine!

When I am finished growing, will I start over and become small again?

Even though you sometimes might wish to be a baby again so that you can be cuddled, it is not possible. Once you have grown, you will live the rest of your life as an adult. Just as children can play and be happy, adults can, too!

Why do we live?

That is a difficult question to answer. People live because they have been given the gift of life. It is each person's responsibility to live a productive life and to try to be happy. You must remember that life is good even though it has many difficulties.

What is happiness?

Happiness is different for everyone. It can be the freedom of being able to come and go as you please. It can be having friends and family to love. For some people, happiness can mean having something to eat and a warm place to sleep every day.

I, my family

Why can't I sleep in the same room as my parents?

When you were a baby, you needed more care than you do now. When you were tiny, your parents had to fill your every need. But now that you are older, it is time to begin a life that is a little more separate from your parents. It is all part of growing up.

How does someone find a husband or a wife?

The way to do that is to open your heart as well as your eyes. There is no magical way to make someone love you. You begin by reaching out and being kind and giving to others. Then, who knows? Love may be returned to you. Many people feel that romantic love comes to you because of fate. Fate is when something happens naturally as if it were always supposed to happen.

Is it bad to like one parent more than the other?

This might happen once in a while especially if you are mad at one of your parents. You also may have more in common with one parent than with the other. Luckily, no one is making you choose a favorite parent. You don't have to feel torn between them. Mothers and fathers are very different from each other. You just love each of them differently, that's all.

Do people ever get married when they are very young or when they are very old?

People are not allowed to get married at a very young age, but there are marriages late in life. For the most part, people get married after they have finished school and are settled into a job.

What is the kind of love that I have for my brother or sister?

As you grow up, you form a bonding kind of love with a brother or sister. It comes from sharing so many experiences for so many years. You play together, read stories together, and laugh and cry together over many, many things. Even when you are mad at your brother or sister, you still have a love for each other that will probably last forever. When you grow up and separate from one another, even this will bring you closer together in your hearts.

Do parents always love their children?

Most parents love their children very much. Some parents, however, know how to love their children better than other parents. A happy home is where parents and children try to get along and build their love over the years.

Do children love their parents forever?

Over the many years that you and your parents know each other, strong bonds are formed. The first people you see and love in the world are your parents. Hopefully, that love will continue to grow and grow. As you get older, something special can happen between you and your mother and father. Besides being your parents, they might even become your friends!

Do parents love each other forever?

Love between a man and a woman is a little bit different. It can last for a short time or it can last a lifetime. It is always wonderful when it lasts! Relationships between men and women depend upon feelings, and feelings can be delicate. Parents will sometimes separate or divorce if their feelings for each other change.

Why do parents get angry with their children?

Some grown-ups are not very patient with youngsters. They do not take the time to see the world through the eyes of their children. They feel that they must rush through the world. If children want to take more time to discover things than parents do, this can irritate the parent.

Do parents ever hit their children?

Yes, some parents become so angry that they get violent. A better way to deal with the problems between a parent and child is through communication, patience, understanding, and love.

Can a child talk back to a parent?

Children should respect their parents and trust that the things that parents do and say are for the good of all. You should not talk back in anger to your parents. You should all sit down and have a heart-to-heart talk to settle the problem.

Why do children have to obey their parents?

Children must obey their parents because parents have the experience and wisdom to know what is best. Obeying your parents can lead to some very fun and exciting adventures!

Can young children spend the day having adventures in new places without any grown-ups?

No, there are too many surprises that can happen. You could get lost. You could get into an accident. You could get kidnapped. You might get hungry and thirsty but have no money. Young children should only go on adventures if there is a trusted grown-up along.

Should children run away from home?

No, that is a very bad idea. Children need to be cared for in the warmth and comfort of their families. The years will pass soon enough when you will be able to go off on your own. You'll be ready to leave home when you are older and better able to provide for your own needs.

Why do grandparents like to talk about the good old days?

The good old days were happy times for grandparents. It feels good to relive fun memories of youthful days. Grandparents can tell you stories about when your parents were little. These stories along with photographs can help you understand the person you are today.

Are grandparents going to die?

Sooner or later everyone must die. It is a part of life. Since your grandparents are much older than you, chances are that you will outlive them. But as long as you and your grandparents have this time together, enjoy each other as much as possible!

Will I be very sad when someone I love dies?

Yes. There is no way to avoid it. You will be sad and cry, but eventually time will heal the sadness. You will begin to feel better. You will even have some laughs when you remember the good times that you had with the person. You will never forget the person, but your life must go on.

Why do people die? There must be death because there has been life. When people are very old, their life forces become tired. These people die quietly, like going to sleep. Sometimes people die from painful illnesses or accidents. This is very difficult to accept and understand.

Why is there a funeral when people die? Since prehistoric times, a ceremony has been conducted to honor a person who has died. The purpose of the ceremony is so that the loved ones can show their respect for a person they have shared things with in life.

When people are buried, what happens to them? Their bodies break down and become one with the earth. In that way, life goes on—only in a different form.

I, others

Why do people live in cities?

People are drawn to cities for jobs, services, and entertainment. Society needs the work and talents of many different people from bakers to bankers. People are social beings. That is, they feel a need to gather in groups to share common interests and feelings. School would not be as much fun without your friends that you see there!

Why do I have to share?

Sharing is a very kind and generous thing to do. When you play with others and share what you have, you don't feel so alone in the world.

Why do I have to be nice to people when I don't want to be?

In order to get along in the world, it is important to have good manners.

Why do I have to be polite?

Being polite makes life easier. You should always remember to say "please," "thank you," "excuse me," "good morning," and so on. It shows that you respect people. They, in turn, will respect you.

What does it mean to behave?

Behaving is when you do your best to be good. This means keeping your room tidy, minding your manners, playing nicely, doing your homework, caring about others, and sharing the things you have.

Why is it so much fun to pretend?

Pretending allows you to discover different ways of being. Playing different characters allows your imagination to run free.

Why is playing "dress up" so much fun?

Feeling what it must be like to be a cat, a monster, or a person from a different place and time is very exciting. It allows you to see the world through different eyes. Dressing in different costumes allows people to dream!

Why don't grown-ups play very much?

Some grown-ups have forgotten how to play. They have become so busy with their jobs and responsibilities that they don't even think about playing anymore. But there are some grown-ups who know a very special secret about life. They know that you're never too old to play. They will always be young at heart.

Do others know when I am telling a lie?

No one knows for sure when you are telling a lie unless they discover the real truth later. Telling lies can lead to trouble. If you tell lies, people will not be able to trust you. They won't know whether to believe you or not, even when you are telling the truth. Pretty soon you'll find yourself without any friends at all.

Do grown-ups always tell the truth?

They try to. They have learned that telling the truth is for the best. Occasionally, adults will tell a lie in order to not hurt someone's feelings. The truth is not easy to find sometimes. One person's version of the truth might be quite different from another's. Then you don't know what to believe. In this case, you'd need to do some research of your own to decide what is true.

Do parents have secrets?

There are some things that parents would rather wait to tell you until you are older. You should be patient and accept this. They will tell you when it is time. If you really need an answer to your question, perhaps your parents can find the words and the way to tell you.

Why can't I watch television all the time?

Too much of anything can get boring! There are other fun things to do besides watching television. You can read a book, play outside, visit with family and friends, play with toys and puzzles, go skating, or play basketball and other sports.

Why do I have to go to bed early?

In order for you to grow big and strong, you need to get plenty of rest. Sleep restores your energy so that you can be active again the next day. You won't be able to enjoy your life if you are tired.

Why do grown-ups say bad words but won't let children say them?

No one should use bad language. Sometimes adults lose control of their emotions, however, and the bad words come out. Grown-ups are not setting a good example for others when they speak this way. It is best to count to ten or go for a walk when you are angry.

Why do children need to learn how to use knives, forks, and spoons?

If you used just your hands to eat, you would make a very big mess. Food would be all over the place. It would be hard to clean the table and your clothes after each meal. Knives, forks, and spoons make mealtime tidy.

Why can't I only eat food that I like?

You must be careful of what you eat. If you eat only sweets, you could ruin your health and your teeth. If you don't eat healthy foods such as fruit and vegetables, you may not grow properly. Have a little bit of a lot of different healthy things rather than a lot of one thing such as dessert.

Why can't I be mean to other children?

If someone makes you mad, there are better ways of dealing with the situation than hitting, biting, or screaming. Try to settle your problems peacefully. Communicate your feelings in words, and you will get better results.

How come grown-ups smoke cigarettes even though they know that it is bad for them?

People sometimes start smoking when they are very young because they want to appear grown up. But smoking cigarettes is addicting. Once you have the habit, it is very hard to stop. It is best to not start smoking in the first place.

Why do people drink alcohol?

Some people drink to relax, but too much alcohol can make you ill. Alcohol is very unhealthy if it is abused. It leads to a disease called alcoholism, which can tear families apart. Drunk drivers also kill innocent people with their cars. Drinking a little bit of alcohol is one thing, but drinking a lot of alcohol can be deadly.

Why do some people waste food when other people are starving?

Our world is a world of the haves and have nots . . . the rich and the poor. But even if you have plenty of food to eat, you still should not waste it. You should appreciate the things that you have and try to help others who are less fortunate.

How do I choose a job?

Have you thought about what you want to be when you grow up? The job that you will have is called your occupation or career. Think of the jobs that interest you. There are many possibilities—a doctor, lawyer, banker, plumber, clothes designer, photographer, artist, chef, dentist, carpenter, and many, many others. Choose what interests you and then study very hard to achieve your goal.

Do I have to work when I grow up?

There is no law that says you have to work. Most people want to, though, so that they can build nice lives for themselves with the money that they earn.

Can children earn money?

It is against the law for small children to work. It is your job to attend school so that you will have the skills to earn money when you are older. There are some ways children can earn a little money if they have the permission of their parents. They can have a paper route, a lemonade stand, sell some things at a yard sale, shovel snow, or mow lawns.

Can children go to jail?

No, because they are too young. Parents are responsible for the mistakes that their children make. If a mistake is a serious one, the police will have to get involved. Sometimes a child might be sent to a special school if he or she cannot behave.

Why is there crime?

Some people want something for nothing, and they break the law to accomplish this. If they are caught, however, they face serious trouble. They can be fined a lot of money and put in jail. Their rights will be taken away, and their lives will be very difficult.

Why are some people unhappy?

There is both happiness and sadness in everyone. People become sad when they can't cope with their problems or if they are sick. If you are sad, you should not give up hope. Happiness might be just around the corner.

Will I learn everything I am to know in school?

No. You will learn many things in school, but life teaches us things everywhere. Grown-ups learn new things every day even though they have been out of school for many years. It is not possible to know everything. However, if you keep your eyes and ears open and if you are curious and want to learn, you can become very wise.

Do I have to like school?

You should try to enjoy your studies. There are many interesting things to learn if you give school a chance. In order to mature, you must learn to think and to communicate. Then you can understand the world a little better and increase your chances to find happiness.

Why do children like to ask so many questions?

Because children are curious, and they like to have the answers to things. This world is very exciting. It is a wonderful feeling to discover and share our world.

Glossary

addicting—habit-forming (p. 54)

blushing—the reddening of the face when a person is embarrassed, shy, or irritated (p. 18)

career—a job or an occupation that people undertake when they have finished their schooling (p. 56)

dreams—a world invented by people as they sleep (p. 12)

dress up—dressing in different costumes and pretending to be somebody other than yourself (p. 46)

fairy tales—stories that teach important things about life in an entertaining and fascinating way (p. 14)

imagination—the creative use of a person's mind to perceive images not existing in reality (p. 46)

manners—behavior that people exhibit in public—good or bad (p. 44)

nightmare—a frightening dream invented by people as they sleep (p. 12)

prehistoric—a long time ago before history was written down (p. 40)

secret—something that a person wants to keep from public knowledge (p. 48)

sharing—the giving of what you have to others (p. 42)

Index

aggression 22
alcohol 54
anger 20, 34
beauty 24
behaving 44
blushing 18
brother 30
career 56
child labor 56
cigarettes 54
cities 42
communication 34
crime 56
crying 16
death 38, 40
depression 20
divorce 32
doctor 16
dolls 12
dreams 12
dress up 46
education 18
explorer 16
fairy tales 14
fate 28
funeral 40
ghosts 14
giants 14
grandparents 38
handicapped 20
happiness 26, 58

hate 24
imagination 46
jealousy 22
job 56
language, bad 50
life 26
love 24
magician 16
manners 44
marriage 30
nightmare 12
occupation 56
ogres 14
parents 30, 32, 34
photographs 8
polite 44
pretending 46
questions 60
romantic love 28
school 60
secret 16
sharing 42
sister 30
smoking 54
sports 22
steam 22
teddy bears 12
television 50
thoughts 16
thumb sucking 18
witches 14

63